THE
Archive Photographs
SERIES

BIRTLEY

HERBERT SOULSBY, BLACKSMITH AT PROUDLOCK'S.

THE
Archive Photographs
SERIES

BIRTLEY

Compiled by
George Nairn and Dorothy Rand

CHALFORD

First published 1997
Copyright © George Nairn and Dorothy Rand, 1997

The Chalford Publishing Company
St Mary's Mill, Chalford,
Stroud, Gloucestershire, GL6 8NX

ISBN 0 7524 0366 4

Typesetting and origination by
The Chalford Publishing Company
Printed in Great Britain by
Bailey Print, Dursley, Gloucestershire

LOOKING NORTH ON THE OLD A1 IN THE EARLY YEARS OF THIS CENTURY.

Contents

BIRTLEY TOWN PRIZE QUARTETTE PARTY, 1908.

Acknowledgements

We have tried, as far as possible, to establish ownership and obtain permission to reproduce photographs, also to check the information which comes from many sources and which we give in good faith.

We would like to acknowledge the works of earlier historians of Birtley and Bewicke Main. Our thanks to all contributors of pictures and information:

Gateshead M.B.C. Libraries and Arts Service, Beamish Photographic Archive, Birtley British Legion, British Aerospace (NPF and ROF), Harcros Durham Chemicals, AEI (Henley Cables), Durham City Library.

Nancy Atkin, George Bell, Tom Cardy, Vera Carty, Will Cavanagh, Derek Charlton, John Dodds, the Elton family, Dorothy Emmerson, Dorothy Hall, Bob Harland, Bob Harris, Doreen Henderson, Claire Humpherson, Alan Hutchinson, Bob Johnson, Brian Kirkup, Colin Lowther, Jack Magee, Mary McColm (nee Kirkup), Tom Nairn, Norma Oliver, Dorothy Prowse (MBE), Dr Alan Richardson, Norman Robson, Harry Roy, John Sanders, Nellie Scott, Liz Smith, Bert Soulsby, Jack Stoker, Shelagh Trusson (nee Hunt), Bob Tuck, Margaret Underwood, Valerie Waggatt, Alan Whitmore, Joyce Whitmore, Winnie Whitmore.

And last, but not least, we would like to thank Gill Nairn and Stan Rand who have had to live with 'The Birtley Book'.

STATION ROAD LOOKING TOWARDS DURHAM ROAD.

Introduction

I started collecting postcards eighteen years ago when I was given a postcard of the 1936 Ravensworth Castle Tattoo. This started my interest in the Ravensworth family and the Castle. I then started collecting postcards of my home town of Chester-le-Street with its own Lambton and Lumley Castle cards.

From these small beginnings my collection has grown to cover most villages and towns in Northumberland and Durham. I specialise in mining and railway cards, and have attended postcard and antique fairs all over the country.

Picture postcards were first used in Great Britain in 1894, and because they record local events and scenes, some long gone, they are particularly suitable as illustrations for local history books.

We are fortunate in having two prolific postcard photographers and publishers, both based in Gateshead, whose work appears in this book. The Johnston family produced the 'Monarch' series of cards from the early 1900s to the late 1940s. Many of the photographs include the photographer's car and they are numbered and titled in the lower left hand corner (see p. 126). S.M. Gibson's cards can be identified by their distinctive white hand-written titles (see p. 35).

George Nairn
July 1997

In 1995 the opportunity arose to work on another book with George Nairn. Researching and writing about social and local history is my favourite occupation so I said 'yes'.

The pictures in this book have come from George Nairn's postcard collection, family albums, industrial archives and public collections. Although not intended as such when taken, every photograph, however ordinary, is an important document in our social history. Studying the pictures, researching written records and sharing people's memories has been a rewarding experience.

Our book, of largely unpublished photographs, is not intended to be a complete history of Birtley, nor can it deal with all aspects of life, because we are restricted by the photographs available. This is a collection of photographs and memories to show how the people and the place have changed, and we hope that you will enjoy this book. Looking at photographs, whether you are young or old, a lifelong resident of Birtley or a newcomer, is an enjoyable way of learning about local history and how we used to live.

Dorothy A. Rand
July 1997

HAVING A GOOD TIME. Whether celebrating a carnival or a Coronation, Birtley people enjoyed dressing up. They are seen here in the 1953 Coronation Fancy Dress Parade. Note the stylish 'Miss Birtley' wearing a swimsuit in the front of the picture.

One
Elisabethville and the Munitions Factories

George Road Entrance, Elizabethville, Birtley. 5146

THE HUTS. The model village of Elisabethville was built in the First World War to house Belgian workers at the National Projectile Factory. The Huts, as the houses were called, were envied by many local people whose own housing was of a much lower standard. Mr Prowse, a representative of the British Government, lived in the end bungalow (centre of photograph) before moving to Durham Road.

TO THE BELGIAN REFUGEES.

RIGHT WELCOME, ❧
LUCKLESS BELGIANS!

RIGHT welcome, luckless Belgians,
  To Britain's sea-girt land!
It is with warmest gratitude
  We grip you by the hand
In sympathetic, heartfelt love,
  And offer you a home,
That, victims of a fiendish Pow'r,
  No longer should you roam
In jeopardy, and destitute,
  Around your countryside.
Thank God, we're able to befriend
  Such heroes proved and tried!

Black crime shall Hist'ry's pen imprint—
  How your quiescent State,
War-free by Treaty pledge, was made
  The butt of wrath and hate
By monstrous tyrants, dastard brutes,
  Of merest shame bereft,
Who deeds of savage heathen wrought,
  Foul murder, outrage, theft!
May One above, Who ruleth o'er
  The boundless universe,
Through vict'ry to the Allied arms,
  These modern Huns disperse!

[COPYRIGHT.]   OSBORNE HEWETT.

BELGIAN REFUGEES. There was great sympathy for the Belgian refugees fleeing from German atrocities, at the same time it was realised that munitions were in short supply. National Projectile Factories were built by private firms and the government working together. In 1915 Armstrong Whitworth agreed to build two factories at Birtley, one to produce shells, the other cartridge cases. Belgian refugees were to be employed at Birtley.

A STRICT REGIME. M. Hubert Debauche, General Manager of the NPF in 1916. The factory was administered by the Belgian government on strict military lines, workers had to wear uniform at work and outside the camp. After a riot on 21 December 1916 caused by the imprisonment of a workman for wearing civilian clothes, discipline was gradually relaxed. More recreation was provided for the workmen and they were allowed to go to more local public houses. The arrival of the men's families had a civilising influence. At its peak, Elisabethville had a population of 6,000, of these 1,200 were children.

A PASS INTO ELISABETHVILLE. A model village, named after Queen Elisabeth of Belgium, was built to house the workers at the National Projectile Factory, who were a mixture of refugees and wounded Belgian soldiers. Elisabethville was self-contained with its own doctors, nurses, teachers and so on. The village was cut off from Birtley by a surrounding fence and local people were not allowed in, except for certain categories of people who had a pass such as this. The first occasion when local people were freely invited into Elisabethville was the Armistice on 11 November 1918. They shared in a torchlight procession and watched the burning of a straw effigy of the Kaiser.

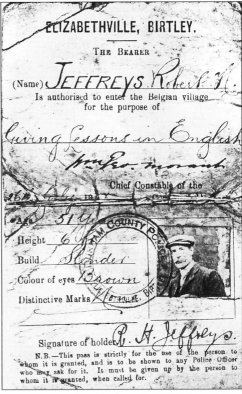

MR A.E. PROWSE. Mr Prowse was the local representative of the Ministry of Munitions and, along with a large administrative staff of clerks, was responsible for housing in Elisabethville. The British also took responsibility for financial aspects of the National Projectile Factory, purchasing raw materials and supplies and paying wages.

THE BELGIAN SCHOOL. Shown here when it was newly built in 1915/16, the school, designed to last for ten years, survived for nearly sixty. Its opening was delayed when three boys – later caught and punished – smashed all the windows. Small coke stoves provided heating when coke was available, but one very cold day pupils were sent home when the ink froze in the inkwells!

GIRLS AT THE BELGIAN SCHOOL. Mr Prowse decided that his children should attend the Belgian School. The reports of Dorothy Prowse (who was a good scholar) show that the usual subjects were taught, plus Hygiene, French and Flemish. The metric system was used which gave the English pupils temporary relief from feet and inches and pounds, shillings and pence.

12

ST MICHAEL'S CHURCH. Belgian clergy looked after the church and cemetery. The chaplains were M. Verpoorten and F. Colbrant, supported by J. Thiry, assistant chaplain and H. Leseck, sacristan. The church stood near the school, it later became the Salvation Army Hall.

THE INTERIOR OF ST MICHAEL'S CHURCH. Surprisingly, for strangers in a strange land, there was a low level of church attendance amongst the Belgians. Lt. Algrain said, 'In Belgium, church-going is political. To go to church means you are a Clerical.'

BUILDING THE FACTORY. This photograph was taken on 26 April 1916 and shows the erection of the building later known as the 6" Shell Shop and North Case Shop.

INSTALLING THE PRESSES. By the end of May 1916 the shell forging presses were being installed. The factory manufactured 8" and 6" high explosive shells and 60 pounder shrapnel shells. Delivery began of the 6" shells in July 1916, followed by the 60 pounders at the end of August, and the 8" shells at the end of September. Other types of shells were produced at other times.

MAINTENANCE. Shells were desperately needed and maximum output was crucial to the success of the war. This photograph shows maintenance on the 8" shell lines in 1916. The open belt drive with unguarded belts would not be allowed by present day health and safety regulations.

BELGIAN WORKERS. Males over fourteen years of age and some young women were employed in the National Projectile Factory. The son of one Belgian worker remembered that his father worked twelve-hour shifts – 7 a.m. to 7 p.m. one week, 7 p.m. to 7 a.m. the next.

FOOD FOR THE GUNS.

FOOD FOR THE GUNS. This is a War Bond Campaign postcard, sold for one penny to raise money for National War Savings Committees Campaigns. It was designed from material supplied by the Ministry of Information and was passed by the Censor. On the original coloured card these slim and elegant ladies are wearing apricot-coloured dresses. That was the official image, the reality was rather different.

A MUNITIONS WORKER AT BIRTLEY. Emmalyne Colpitts was photographed at the end of the war in the uniform she wore as a munitions worker at Birtley. Women did jobs traditionally done by men. The middle and upper classes were involved in charity work, nursing and refugee work.

NATIONAL PROJECTILE FACTORY WORKERS, 1917. Harriet Lope is third left in the front row, and fourth left is Hilda Johnson. She inspected shells by shining a lamp up the middle. A number of the workers are wearing black armbands.

BIRTLEY C.C.F. LADIES FOOTBALL TEAM, 1917-18. The Cartridge Case Factory Team played for enjoyment and also raised money for charity. Their home ground was the Chester-le-Street cricket ground. The tiger skin rug in the foreground appears in other photographs, such as one taken at Armstrong's factory which is in Beamish Photographic Archive. Presumably the rug was the photographer's 'prop'.

JULIEN DEDRIE'S SHOP. Behind this door lay the Elisabethville photographer's shop where a number of the pictures in this book were produced. We owe a debt of gratitude to Julien Dedrie for his legacy of images of not only Elisabethville, but also of Birtley itself.

BOULEVARD PRINCE LEOPOLD. Resident photographer, Julien Dedrie took this view which looks up to one of the gateways of Elisabethville, conveniently opposite the Three Tuns – here spelt wrongly as 'Tons'. The housing in Elisabethville provided a higher standard of accommodation than many local residents enjoyed, e.g. flush toilets and electric lights. The Belgian village consisted of hostels for single men and two sizes of furnished cottages with gardens for families.

18

MISS CATHERINE BLYTHE. A Gala Evening was held in Elisabethville on Wednesday 10 July 1918 at 8 p.m., entrance was one shilling. Miss Blythe, who also played for the silent films at Bolams, was a star performer in both halves of the programme. Other fund-raising galas of a different nature were also held, such as the Neptune Swimming Club Gala near Lumley Castle in June 1918. Entertainment was by 'Fanfare' the Belgian Military Band composed of fifty discharged soldiers. The gala was held in aid of Belgian prisoners of war in Germany.

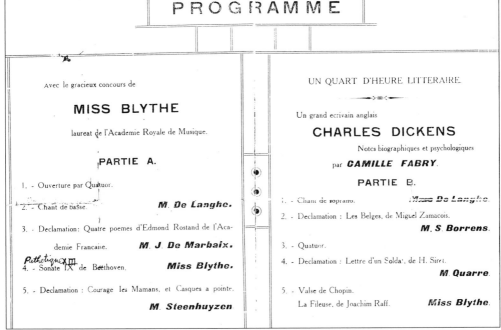

PROGRAMME

Avec le gracieux concours de

MISS BLYTHE

laureat de l'Academie Royale de Musique.

PARTIE A.

1. - Ouverture par Quatuor.

2. - Chant de basse. **M. De Langhe.**

3. - Declamation: Quatre poemes d'Edmond Rostand de l'Academie Francaise. **M. J. De Marbaix.**

Pathetique XII
4. - Sonate IX de Beethoven. **Miss Blythe.**

5. - Declamation : Courage les Mamans, et Casques a pointe.
M. Steenhuyzen.

UN QUART D'HEURE LITTERAIRE.

Un grand ecrivain anglais

CHARLES DICKENS

Notes biographiques et psychologiques

par **CAMILLE FABRY.**

PARTIE B.

1. - Chant de soprano. *Miss De Langhe.*

2. - Declamation : Les Belges, de Miguel Zamacois.
M. S. Borrens.

3. - Quatuor.

4. - Declamation : Lettre d'un Soldat, de H. Siret.
M. Quarre.

5. - Valse de Chopin.
La Fileuse, de Joachim Raff. **Miss Blythe.**

THE PROGRAMME. This is Catherine Blythe's programme with her handwritten note indicating which piece of Beethoven's music she would play. The Gala Evening was held in Cheval Blanc (The White Horse) a cafe aimed at reproducing a Bruxelloise atmosphere. The Birtley Press printed the programme.

JEU DE BALLE. A favourite Sunday afternoon activity takes place in front of the Three Tuns. It is a game played in Belgian French speaking regions and in the south of Flanders. Two teams of five hurl a small leather ball the size of a golf ball between them.

FANFARE. This was a brass band formed in 1917 composed of disabled soldiers. A symphony orchestra had been founded in December 1916.

A HEAVEN ON EARTH. Belgian soldiers and their families, 1917. Many Belgians were very happy in Elisabethville and regarded it as a happy haven after being war refugees. Frans Waerie wrote of his parents, 'At Birtley my parents lived in a wooden hut. This hut, provided with all conveniences, was very commodious … and well supplied with the necessary furniture. For the simple people they were, for my father who came back from the trenches and mother who had lived through a lot of privations in Belgium, this humble house was somewhat like a 'heaven on earth'. At Birtley they were never short of anything. For my parents, Durham and surroundings was the most beautiful area they'd ever seen in their lives.'

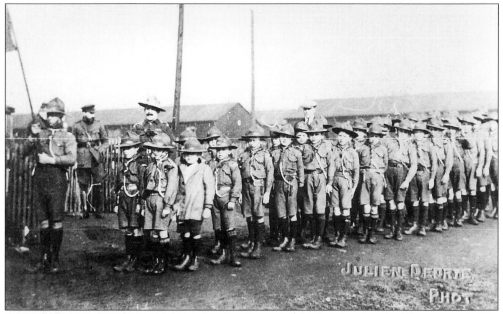

BELGIAN BOY SCOUTS. Julien Dedrie's embossed stamp is very clear on this postcard. The scout master was M. Blondeel from Ghent. The boy scouts put on a play at the Birtley Hall, it was in Flemish and was about the Germans and the Kaiser. All the parents were very proud of their sons.

A FAMILY PHOTOGRAPH. Charles Vieren is the boy scout and his little brother is wearing a miniature army uniform. The soldier is Charles' uncle, on leave from the Front.

THE CEMETERY. In 1916 a field adjacent to Lamesely Lane was set aside for a Belgian cemetery. There were thirteen war graves and some civilian graves. During the 1926 Strike unemployed men had the remunerative but unpleasant job of exhuming some of the bodies to be returned to Belgium.

THE ANGUS-SANDERSON CAR. At the end of 1919 the National Projectile Factory was sold to the coachbuilding firm of Angus-Sanderson. Their 14.3 h.p. composite car was produced at Birtley from 1919 to 1921 and the completed cars were often seen leaving the factory for a test run. Local people were resentful of the fact that the firm rented half of the 'Huts' for their workforce and Angus-Sanderson attempted to overcome this hostility by donating prize money for charitable events and promoting gatherings in Birtley.

REASSURING THE PUBLIC. The Angus-Sanderson was an attractive car costing £450, the Princess Royal owned one. Unfortunately there was a waiting time of up to one year. The car was made by the American method of mass production – component parts were sent to Birtley to be assembled – but supplies were often delayed. *The Autocar* ran this advertisement in 1920 to reassure the public by 'camera evidence' that cars were being produced. The firm transferred to Hendon (1921-27), becoming bankrupt due to competition from the cheaper Morris and Ford cars. The NPF building became a Government Training Centre for a while then was closed until it re-opened as the Royal Ordnance Factory in 1936.

A WEDDING IN ELISABETHVILLE. May Kitching (who delivered milk with a pony and cart for Black's Farm) and Frederick Francis from Coundon Station were married on 24 December 1927 at St John's church, Birtley. The photographer turned up on 25 December, just as everyone had sat down to Christmas dinner! The two older bridesmaids are missing from the photograph as they had gone home the previous day. The background is one of the single men's hostels.

THE END OF THE HUTS. The Belgians left in 1919 and the contents of the huts were sold off. The *Daily Mail* described the sale on 26 May 1919 as, 'the largest furniture sale on record.' Some Birtley children managed to 'cadge' things from the departing Belgians, such as clocks which were too difficult to carry. One family still has a dictionary which belonged to a Belgian. The Huts were renamed and let by the Council, one resident remembers paying eleven shillings a week for a four-roomed hut in 1926. By the 1930s these dwellings were rather dilapidated and had outlived their predicted life of ten years. J.B. Priestley in his *English Journey* of 1934 described Elisabethville as, 'A nightmare place that seemed to have been constructed out of small army huts and unwanted dog kennels, all sprawling in the muck outside some gigantic works.' Here we see demolition in progress.

STAFF OF THE SHELL MACHINE SHOP. These Royal Ordnance Factory workers were photographed, for security reasons, at the end of the Second World War. After each long shift, spot checks were carried out and certain workers were taken aside to be searched. Despite this, some shells did find their way into people's homes. Passes were shown going in and out of the factory.

A WINNING TEAM. The First Aid Team at the ROF Birtley travelled to London and competed with Ministry of Defence First Aid Teams from all over the country. They are shown here with some of their awards in 1958. Left to right: Joe Bonney, Dave Ridley, Fred Chapman, Wilson Weddle and Alan Whitmore.

Two
Streets and Buildings

High Row, Bewicke Main.   1050

HIGH ROW, BEWICKE MAIN. Bewicke Main was a village near Birtley which appeared with the opening and disappeared with the closing of the colliery. There were eighty-three houses in five groups – Cross Row, Short Row, Long Row, High Row and The Square. They were lit by oil lamps and candles until 1910 when gas lighting was installed. The houses varied in size but it is known that up to fourteen people lived in one of the smaller houses in Short Row. The smaller houses were built back to back, so only had one door; only the Long and High Rows had two doors. High Row was for officials. There were two bedrooms, a sitting room, a kitchen and a wash house. All the houses had brick floors and yards. The long gardens enabled the miners to grow fruit and vegetables for consumption and competition and some families kept hens and pigs. After the colliery closed in 1932 the population of Bewicke Main dwindled and squatters occupied some houses which by then were becoming dangerous due to subsidence.

PERKINS' MONUMENT. Edward Moseley Perkins lived in Birtley Hall and was a partner in the Birtley Iron Company and part owner of Birtley and Ouston Collieries. He held many public offices and following his death in 1871 this monument was unveiled on Stock Hill in 1874. The Birtley Iron Company made the railings surrounding the monument, but they were removed during the Second World War.

THE FUNNIEST MONUMENT OF COUNTY DURHAM.
Nikolaus Pevsner, writing about the Buildings of England in 1953, described the Perkins' Monument: 'In the Square, the funniest monument of County Durham, to Col. E. Moseley Perkins, 1874, white marble, as naive as a Staffordshire figure.' It was, however, a favourite place to meet and Nellie Ramsey and Edie Fenton are posing against the railings.

TALBOT COTTAGES. Built by the Birtley Iron Company for its officials, these picturesque cottages bear the initials and family crest of Augustus Henry Hunt. The name 'Talbot' is from the Talbot dogs – hounds used for hunting – on the Hunt family crest.

BLACK FELL ROAD. On the left of this card posted in 1913 is the RAOB Club, then Grove Cottages and South Terrace. The Rose and Shamrock is on the right and the Black Fell Engine House is on the horizon.

MONUMENT TERRACE. Jacques Nihoul, a Belgian, wrote on this Birtley Press postcard at 9.30 a.m. on 20 November 1916, and sent it to his parents in Glamorgan. The original railings have a most attractive pattern.

SCHOOL HOUSE, BIRTLEY LANE. Valerie Waggatt sketched this house which has had various occupants, including Deaconess Mary A. Butterworth in 1908, and a church organist who was also a piano tuner. The Deary sisters ran a school here. One sister was later in charge of Birtley telephone exchange.

THE AVENUE. When The Avenue was first built there was an iron gate at the top and a wooden gate at the bottom. The gates were symbolically closed once a year to indicate The Avenue – a prestigious address – was private property. A trough once stood where The Avenue joined the main road. It bore the inscription 'Pro Bono Publico' (for the benefit of the people) which is the motto of Birtley Town Council. The trough was often dry, so when The Avenue was built it was put at the foot of the Red Lion bank. In 1915 it was moved to a more convenient position. (See p. 126)

BIRTLEY LANE. Taken early in this century, this Johnston postcard shows how the road used to be divided. On the left are T. Marsh's confectionery shop and the Moulder's Arms. Straight ahead is a lodge of Birtley Hall at the top of Harras Bank.

ESK TERRACE. Burnetts built Esk Terrace and Egton Terrace. The family came from Egton in Yorkshire, near the River Esk. Ingleside House (Dr Philipson's house) is next to the Big Tree, a favourite boundary marker and meeting place.

EGTON TERRACE. Cyclists in trouble are photographed against this neat terrace with its railing-topped garden walls. In 1979 two nuns from the Congregation of the Daughters of Jesus moved into Hawthorn House, No. 9, Egton Terrace in order to carry out pastoral work in the area.

ST JOHN'S PLACE. Whitened window sills and steps were a matter of pride to housewives as this photograph shows. St John's Place was demolished and replaced by the Arndale Terrace shops.

DURHAM ROAD. The steps of St John's Place can be seen on the left. Traces of the original shop fronts, on the right, can still be seen – detective work such as this is rewarding and interesting. The people on this photograph would be surprised by the volume of traffic on the same road today.

CROW ROW. These houses have been demolished but their situation at the end of Egton Terrace is indicated by the spire of St Joseph's church which appears above a roof on the right of the picture.

Council Houses, Birtley. 5661

THE COUNCIL HOUSES. This postcard was 'Specially reproduced for R.U. Low, Post Office, Birtley', by R. Johnston and Son, Gateshead in their Monarch Series. After the First World War there was a great need to build new houses, as none had been built during the war and much of the older property had deteriorated into slums. The new houses relieved overcrowding and provided indoor toilets, bathrooms and electric lighting, resulting in healthier people with a higher standard of living. The main north-south telecommunications system can be seen on this road which was the A1 before the bypass was built.

BROOK TERRACE. This Gibson card posted in 1918 shows these impressive houses of three storeys plus an attic. Brook Terrace can be seen in the background of the picture of the unveiling of the War Memorial. (See p. 108)

MORRIS STREET. The flats in Morris Street and Jones Street were built by the Bolam Brothers. A few houses at the George Street end of Jones Street were built by the Co-op and were slightly bigger due to extra ground being available.

PERKINS' MEMORIAL HOMES. Named after the famous Perkins family these homes were built in 1905 to accommodate eight people. The man who conceived the idea of Aged Miners' Homes was Joseph Hopper and the scheme celebrated its centenary in 1997.

TRIUNE COTTAGES. Isaac and Frances Fenton stand outside their home around 1910. The cottages were on Durham Road, opposite the Birtley Hall. The sign says 'Fireman'. Early attempts at fire fighting were slow compared to the fire service of today. A fire bell stood in a garden at the bottom of The Avenue, behind The Hanlon. The hand-drawn engine and fire fighting equipment were kept in the village, at one time they were in the old engine house near Birtley Old Hall.

STATION ROAD. This unusual view shows the entrance to Burnett's yard on the left, now the premises of Windows and Conservatories North East Ltd. During the Second World War a Bren gun carrier on a practice run demolished some railings and damaged a building just beyond the large house on the left.

THE STATION HOTEL. Taken from an early Auty glass negative, this photograph shows the now vandalised building in its original condition.

THE GROVE. Possibly built around 1870, with the lodge known as Grove Cottage added twenty years later, this house was in private hands until 1953. One famous occupant was Lancelot Moses who gave the bandstand to the people of Birtley (see p. 114). The greenhouse and distinctive fencing feature is in the background of several of the photographs in this book. In 1953 The Grove was sold to the Parish Council.

THE KIRKUP FAMILY AT LEAFIELD. The boy on this photograph, dating from around 1900, is Philip Kirkup. He went on to have a distinguished military career and unveiled Birtley's War Memorial in 1923 (see p. 108). Philip's brother, Major Ernest Kirkup lived at Leafield when he was a mining engineer for Pelaw Main Collieries. His contract of employment in 1918 gave him an annual salary of £700 plus £350 per annum to cover gardeners' and chauffeurs' wages, and the purchase and upkeep of a car. He had the use of Leafield and two lodges, free of rent, rates, taxes, lighting and water charges. The owners maintained the outside of the house and lodges, and redecorated the interiors from time to time.

BIRTLEY OLD HALL. This stood just past St John's church, over the waggonway. Above the door was the inscription 'John Emmerson 1692'. The Hall was badly damaged by fire and had to be pulled down. One resident in the 1890s was R. Auton, Railway Inspector. The photograph, which has been damaged, shows the Hall decorated with flags and bunting.

BIRTLEY HALL. This simple four-square classical house, set in a wooded estate, was designed by John Dobson for J. Warwick, and completed in 1815. The Hall overlooked Birtley Iron Works and many owners were also managers at the works, including G. Skipsey in 1828, Benjamin Thompson in 1832, John Hine Hunt in 1851, and Edward Perkins in 1865. In 1906 the last occupant was Henry Murton, the Newcastle sports outfitter. The Hall was demolished around 1916.

THE POLICE STATION. This stood on Durham Road next to the Wesleyan chapel. In 1925 William Bell was the sergeant in charge of eight constables. An earlier police house and lock-up was at the end of St John's Place and the adjacent road was known as Polis's Bank. Sergeant Gray was the first person to live above the new station when it opened.

BLACK FELL SANATORIUM. The satisfied patient who sent this card in 1915 wrote, 'Am keeping champion and have been benefited a great deal by the treatment here. Will soon be home ready for work or possibly for the Army. Treatment is practically eating and sleeping. Very good grub.' The Sanatorium was considered to have been built in a very healthy area. After the war it was used as an Isolation Hospital in the Smallpox epidemic.

Three
When We Were Young

The Schools, Bewicke Main. 4058

BEWICKE MAIN SCHOOLS. The Birtley Iron Company built these schools in 1873 to accommodate 120 infants, juniors and seniors. Each of the three rooms had a huge open fire with a large, square fireguard. Alderman Ned Cowen was the best known pupil of Bewicke Main Schools. He paid 2d a week to attend, and left in 1903, aged twelve, having obtained his Labour Certificate. He became a miner and did a great deal to help his fellow miners. The schools closed on 13 November 1931.

ORCHARD STREET SUNDAY SCHOOL. Girls of the Orchard Street Sunday School pose in their Sunday best. The age range here is wide, as children were taken, or sent, to Sunday School from an early age. The Orchard Street Primitive Methodist chapel was erected in 1867, at a cost of £700, and the Sunday Schools were at the back of the chapel separated by a removable partition.

A SUNDAY SCHOOL TABLEAU. Nellie Scott (nee Hudson), born in 1897, is third from the right in the back row. The white sticks are props for a tableau, and the girls practised for months. The lady in the centre of the three adults at the back is Mrs Soulsby, the Minister's wife.

A GARDEN PARTY AT THE VICARAGE. The tableaux were staged in the grounds of St John's vicarage, and this time it is the spectators who are photographed. The blur in the bottom left of the picture is a child whirling round too quickly for the shutter speed of the camera.

PIRATES AT BIRTLEY! Parents and friends are a guaranteed audience when children perform. This group of junior actors includes Norman Flowers with a dagger between his teeth and the venue is again the grounds of the vicarage. The cloche hats worn by the girls and ladies in the background are typical of the 1920s.

BIRTLEY GIRLS GUILDRY. This was based at Station Road chapel. Amongst the leaders on this photograph are Mrs Coulthard, Mrs Bailey and Mrs Kirtley. The girls Guildry (motto – 'Wise unto that which is good.') was formed in 1900 as a Christian uniformed organisation. Founded in Scotland as an interdenominational and international movement, its varied activities were aimed at helping girls to become mature Christian women. There was a strong emphasis on service to others and programmes were provided for four age groups – the wide age group is evident in the photograph. The Girls Guildry was amalgamated with the Girls Brigade in July 1965.

BIRTLEY BOYS BRIGADE. Taken during the Second World War, the 1st Birtley Boys Brigade are at Station Road chapel. The captain was Jimmy Knox and the officers were Mr Gray, Mr Coulthard, Mr Stobbs and Mr Gallon. Alan Whitmore, eighth from the left in the back row, played tenor drum in the band and remembers going to camp at Slaley. Founded by William Alexander Smith in Glasgow in 1883 with the motto of 'Sure and Stedfast', the object of the Boys Brigade was the advancement of Christ's Kingdom amongst boys. Activities included drill, competing for badges, playing in the band and going to annual camp, as well as attending Bible Class or Sunday School. Uniformed youth organisations were very popular between the wars and a dependable source of income for a photographer. Most people in the group would buy at least one postcard, and a framed enlargement might be ordered for the HQ.

BIRTLEY LANE COUNCIL SCHOOL. The school opened in 1860 as a National School and had several additions. Children of Class 5 pose for this photograph, the original is card-mounted. Many parents could not afford to buy these school photographs. Nellie Scott attended this school until George Street School opened in 1908, and it was there she attended her first school assembly. The Birtley Lane School had no assembly hall at this time, and the curate visited each class in turn. One headmaster, Mr Little, applied a large cricket bat to pupils who were late for school.

DRILL AT BIRTLEY LANE SCHOOL, 1928. Drill was in fashion earlier in the century. Each child did exactly the same action at the same time, working to the teacher's shouted instructions. There were often no concessions made to special clothing, the boys appear to be wearing sandshoes but most are restricted by a shirt and tie. They were practising for a drill display at Chester-le-Street. The Church Institute is in the background, it was the venue for large gatherings such as charity balls for the RVI and Masonic Lodge Meetings. It was demolished after the Second World War.

GOOD ATTENDANCE REWARDED. School registers were carefully checked and good attendance was rewarded in various ways. At Birtley Lane School the 'Never Absent Group, 1929-30' each received a copy of this postcard, 'With H.E. Peadon's compliments'. The original of this card was given to Norman Flowers who also went on to become a teacher. Norman is standing next to Mr Peadon and is wearing a jacket and tie. Jackie Horne stands next to Norman and Marjorie Flowers is second left in the middle row.

BIRTLEY LANE SCHOOL FOOTBALL TEAM, 1931-32. The teachers are, left to right: Mr Wilkinson, Mr Peadon (head) and Tim Soulsby who played for Newcastle United. The captain holding the football is Richard Baldwin.

RAVENSWORTH TERRACE SCHOOL, 1924. This infants school also opened in 1860. Class 1 boys, wearing typical elementary school dress, are looking rather solemn. Their teacher is Miss Armstrong. Many are wearing boots – most working class children wore them as many streets were not made up and became quagmires after heavy rain. Boots were often repaired at home and in times of great financial difficulty might even be soled with cardboard. Some children went barefoot in the 1926 Strike.

GEORGE STREET COUNCIL SCHOOLS. Chester-le-Street Rural District Councillor, Mr R.H. Lonsdale performed the opening ceremony in 1908 and the building closed as a school in July 1996.

STAFF AT GEORGE STREET SCHOOL. Thought to be taken at the time the school opened in 1908, the staff pose for this formal photograph. Mr Jeffreys, the headmaster, is seated in the middle of the front row. Miss Dalton, wearing a flower on her blouse, sits next to him. The rigid discipline and formality of school life in 1908 contrasts strongly with the type of education in the school when it closed in 1996.

BIRTLEY NEW COUNCIL STANDARD 3. This is the photographer's identification of the class at George Street School, possibly in 1909. Liza Bolam holds the board. Florrie Whitmore is standing next to Mr Jeffreys who lived at No. 17, The Avenue. The teacher is Miss Dalton.

JENNIE AND WINNIE WHITMORE, C. 1916. Jennie and Winnie, daughters of Philip Whitmore, fishmonger, lived in Morris Street and were pupils at George Street School. Jennie, on the left, born 1905, worked as a private nurse in the National Children's Homes and trained at Selly Oak, Birmingham. Winnie, born 1908, was in service in Leeds and was later housemaid to Col. Joicey at Blenkinsopp Hall. During the Second World War she was in the stores of Birtley Engineering Works where scout cars were made (see p. 99). She then worked as a hairdresser in Birtley until her retirement.

BIRTLEY COUNCIL SCHOOL FOOTBALL TEAM. Shown here in 1911, the team were runners-up in the Chester-le-Street League and winners of the Shafto Cup. William Arthur Dawson, at the right end of the back row, is wearing his 'England' cap presented by Newcastle United. He played for England in the English Schools' Football Association, England v Scotland International Match at St James' Park on Saturday 13 May 1911. Will also played in the All-England School Shield at the Birtley Ground on 29 April 1911, when the ball was presented by Mr Gailles of the Station Hotel, Birtley.

A WARTIME WOODWORK LESSON. This *Newcastle Chronicle* photograph was taken during the early part of the Second World War – later there was no wood to spare for woodwork lessons. The lesson was at Birtley East Secondary Modern School and Mr Lightfoot was the teacher. On the extreme left is Billy Tinkler whose father was the local 'bobby'. Bob Waistell is on the extreme right, and Alan Whitmore is next to him.

CANTEEN STAFF AT BIRTLEY EAST SCHOOL. The school, opened in 1933, was set in five acres and cost £17,988 to build. This photograph, taken around 1947, shows the canteen staff. Mrs Eva Whitmore, second from the right in the front row, retired as meals supervisor in 1967 after twenty-five years service. At a special assembly Mr Bragg, the headmaster, presented Mrs Whitmore with a silver teapot and jug and the head girl, Lynne Marsh, presented a bouquet.

CELEBRATING THE JUBILEE. The children of Birtley East Nursery celebrated the Queen's Silver Jubilee in 1977 with a Fancy Dress Parade, here photographed by the *Northern Echo*. Mrs Dorothy Emmerson was in charge of the nursery which opened in 1972. There were places for fifty children of three years to school age.

CALENDAR 1950

	JAN	FEB	MAR
S	1 8 15 22 29	.. 5 12 19 26	.. 5 12 19 26
M	2 9 16 23 30	.. 6 13 20 27	.. 6 13 20 27
Tu	3 10 17 24 31	.. 7 11 21 28	.. 7 14 21 28
W	4 11 18 25	1 8 15 22	1 8 15 22 29
Th	5 12 19 26	2 9 16 23	2 9 16 23 30
F	6 13 20 27	3 10 17 24	3 10 17 24 31
S	7 14 21 28	4 11 18 25	4 11 18 25

	APRIL	MAY	JUNE
S	- 2 9 16 23 30	.. 7 14 21 28	.. 4 11 18 25
M	- 3 10 17 24	1 8 15 22 29	.. 5 12 19 26
Tu	- 4 11 18 25	2 9 16 23 30	.. 6 13 20 27
W	- 5 12 19 26	3 10 17 24 31	.. 7 14 21 28
Th	- 6 13 20 27	4 11 18 25	1 8 15 22 29
F	- 7 14 21 28	5 12 19 26	2 9 16 23 30
S	1 8 15 22 29	6 13 20 27	3 10 17 24

	JULY	AUG	SEP
S	- 2 9 16 23 30	.. 6 13 20 27	.. 3 10 17 24
M	- 3 10 17 24 31	.. 7 14 21 28	.. 4 11 18 25
Tu	- 4 11 18 25	1 8 15 22 29	.. 5 12 19 26
W	- 5 12 19 26	2 9 16 23 30	.. 6 13 20 27
Th	- 6 13 20 27	3 10 17 24 31	.. 7 14 21 28
F	- 7 14 21 28	4 11 18 25	1 8 15 22 29
S	1 8 15 22 29	5 12 19 26	2 9 16 23 30

	OCT	NOV	DEC
S	1 8 15 22 29	.. 5 12 19 26	.. 3 10 17 24 31
M	2 9 16 23 30	.. 6 13 20 27	.. 4 11 18 25
Tu	3 10 17 24 31	.. 7 14 21 28	.. 5 12 19 26
W	4 11 18 25	1 8 15 22 29	.. 6 13 20 27
Th	5 12 19 26	2 9 16 23 30	.. 7 14 21 28
F	6 13 20 27	3 10 17 24	1 8 15 22 29
S	7 14 21 28	4 11 18 25	2 9 16 23 30

FUNDRAISING FOR A SCHOOL FILM CLUB. Scent cards were a popular way for organisations to raise funds at this time. This one, probably sold before Christmas 1949 at 2d, was from Phul-Nana Perfumery and featured an exotic dancer on the other side. The cards were purchased in multiples of one thousand, and sold in large numbers. Ladies put them in their handbags and underwear drawers.

Four
Shopping

JOSEPH ENGLISH. This photograph of the president of Birtley District Co-operative Society is taken from the Jubilee Handbook of 1911.

BIRTLEY TINPLATE WORKS. The CWS acquired the Birtley Tinplate Works in 1908 and closed them sixty years later. This artist's impression shows their location to the north of Station Lane, along the east side of the main NER line. Domestic tinware was made in large quantities with over five hundred different articles being produced. Industrial flour bins and shoots for the storage of all kinds of flour, meal and grain were also manufactured. The CWS Jubilee book of 1913 states that the number of employees was thirty-nine.

MR AND MRS GEORGE MELVILLE. Mr George Melville was night watchman at the old Co-op store on Harras Bank and witnessed its destruction by fire on Christmas morning, 1900. Next day he took his grand-daughter Nellie (now Mrs Scott) to examine the remains of the building. Sifting through the ashes with his walking stick he found a shilling coin. He had a hole bored in it so that he could wear it on his watch chain as a memento, and it can be seen on this photograph.

DURHAM ROAD, BIRTLEY

BUILDING THE NEW CO-OP. Before the Harras Bank Co-op was destroyed by fire at the end of 1900, the Birtley House Estate had been purchased, so trading resumed from there 'within a few hours'. The foundation stone of the new Durham Road premises was laid on 24 August 1901 and the building was completed by 28 August 1903. This hand-coloured postcard shows the stores under construction.

CO-OP STAFF. Nellie Scott is second from the left in the front row, she went straight from school to work in the greengrocery department. Her bearded grandfather, George Melville is behind her. As night watchman at the new Co-op building, he patrolled at night with two Great Danes and a revolver!

CO-OPERATIVE STORES, BIRTLEY. The completed premises were magnificent and they provided everything 'from the cradle to the grave'. There was a butchery department, grocery, greengrocery, millinery, shoes, cafe and cake shop, drapery, furniture and hardware departments and a dairy. Upstairs was the tailoring department, a billiard hall, the small hall, a union room and cash and other offices. The Co-op allowed credit to miners on strike. An advertisement by Birtley Co-op in 1921 said, 'It is well known that we were among the first to assist during the recent dispute. We ask for increased loyalty.'

BIRTLEY STORES. Most people went to 'The Store' and still remember their check number. This postcard shows the building from a different angle. The steeply-roofed building next to the Co-op was a lodge of Birtley House, it is now Bimbi's restaurant. On the extreme left of the picture is the Danish Dairy.

CO-OP DELIVERY CART. A large number of vehicles delivered food and other products, the average small dealer had a horse and cart and the Co-op had quite a number. The Co-op horses were kept in the former stables of Birtley House. Traces of the tiled walls of the stables and the cobbled stable yard can be seen behind the Masonic Hall. Joseph Lightburn is seen here with his immaculately groomed and decorated horse.

CUSTOMER CARE IN 1911. Nothing but the best for the members of Birtley Co-op! Customers of branches at Outson, Fatfield, Wrekenton, New Washington and Washington Station were able to visit the Jubilee Exhibition at the central premises in a motor charabanc. This form of transport, with an average speed of 12 mph, was the latest novelty.

52   *Birtley Co-operative Society's Jubilee.*

MOTOR CHAR-A-BANCS

WILL LEAVE THE BRANCH
PREMISES, AT INTERVALS,

—— ON ——

SATURDAY, July 1st,
WEDNESDAY, July 5th,
AND
SATURDAY, July 8th.

FARE **3d.** FARE

EACH JOURNEY.

THE CO-OP DAIRY VAN. Bob Marshall won second prize for his decorated van in the Co-op's Golden Jubilee Celebrations of 1911. Elaborate plans for this week included an exhibition in the skating rink, band concerts, exhibitions and competitions in the Co-op Hall. The procession of horses and vehicles was on Wednesday 5 July 1911. Members were given a souvenir tray engraved with a view of the central premises.

THE SILVER LINK. Bob Marshall is seen again during the Birtley Carnival of 1936. Lack of money meant most people could not afford to go away on holiday, so local events such as the carnival and 'Holiday at Home' weeks were well supported.

LOOKING AFTER THE CUSTOMER. This horse-drawn van, built by the CWS to exhibit in the Royal Show in Newcastle in 1935, was in use until 1950. An unusual feature was the side door which made it a walk-in mobile shop. Note the pneumatic tyres, headlights and adverts – 'Birtley Co-op for Choice, Quality and Efficiency.' Horse-drawn transport existed alongside motor transport in the 1930s and '40s because for short journeys with frequent stops, a horse was more efficient.

MR COATES AND HIS DELIVERY VAN. An advertisement of 1961: 'Birtley District Co-operative Society Ltd, Central Premises at Birtley and Washington, Branches through the district. Travelling Shops cover all areas. Why not give us a trial. We offer Personal Attention, Quality and Service, Complete Satisfaction and Full Dividend on all purchases.'

Birtley District Co-op. Society, Ltd.

.DURING CARNIVAL WEEK SEE OUR

Furniture....
DISPLAYS

WE ARE THE CHEAPEST IN THE DISTRICT.

BEDROOM SUITES : : FROM £8/8/0
BEDSTEAD TO MATCH : £1/12/6
THREE-PIECE REXINE SUITE £9/10/0
FLOOR COVERING FROM 1/3 PER SQ. YD.
LINOLEUM : : FROM 1/9 PER SQ. YARD.
CYCLES : : FROM £3/19/6.
PRAMS From £2/16/6. CARETTES From 10/-

May we remind you, while you are enjoying this Summer Carnival
that Winter is ahead. **Are you prepared for the Winter Fun ?**

WHAT ABOUT A
WIRELESS SET, RADIOGRAM, GRAMOPHONE, PIANO, or
ANY OTHER INSTRUMENT.

BIRTLEY CO-OP ADVERTISEMENT. The Jubilee Carnival Programme of 1935 carried this advertisement.

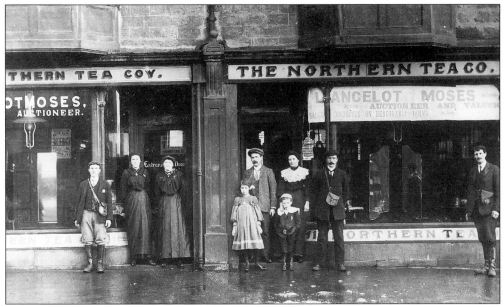

THE NORTHERN TEA COMPANY. Lancelot Moses, who lived in The Grove, was an auctioneer and valuer, and also owned the Northern Tea Company. His sales were, 'conducted on reasonable terms' according to the notice on the window. It seemed that this photograph was taken in winter, as slush appears to be lying on the pavement.

W. COLLINS, BUTCHER. This shop, one of several owned by the family, was at No. 28, Durham Road. Here Mrs Hannah Eleanor Collins (Nellie) poses in the doorway in the 1920s. Ned Cowen recalled that Tuesday was 'killing day' at the Birtley butchers, and that the women of Bewicke Main would go for fresh meat.

ARE YOU LOW? Robert Usher Low who had the post office and the Rexall Pharmacy (now the Northern Rock on Durham Road) could help you. His van advertises the fact that he is sole agent for Rexall's Remedies. These and other famous patent medicines extravagantly claimed to cure many diseases and restore vitality.

BIRTLEY IRONMONGERY STORES. Mr Kay stands at the doorway of his shop in Harraton Terrace around 1900. An amazing variety of goods needed for everyday living was sold in shops such as these. Even the mangle bears the name of Mr Kay who was the originator of Kay's Trips (see p. 122).

J. WHITMORE AND SON, FRUITERERS. Ernie Stott and Ernie Whitmore in about 1910. When the Volunteers' Bus visited Birtley in 1914 they deserted the horse and cart and joined up. Neither of them came back from the war.

YES, WE HAVE SOME BANANAS! Whitmore's shop at No. 36, Durham Road promotes Fyffe's bananas – 5 for 6d. The decorated window displays a profusion of other goods for sale, a wreath is hanging up, and a basket of potatoes is in the doorway. Roy Whitmore, his sister Rita and assistant Nancy Blacklock pose for this photograph, probably in the late 1920s.

W.F. ELTON, BOOT REPAIRER. This is Elton's original shop which was located at the south end of Durham Road, next to what is now Komatsu car park. Walter Frederick Elton was gassed during the First World War and following his discharge he took a course in cobbling in 1919. He started a boot and shoe repair business in Chester-le-Street, then Birtley. The Elton family still have shops in both places, although their present shop in Birtley is now at No. 31, Durham Road which still has its original frontage. Left to right: Hughie Timney, -?-, John Frederick Elton, -?-, Ephraim Wilkinson.

G.R. HUNTER, GENERAL DEALER. Harry and Jenny Hunter took this shop over from Shaws in 1922. The photographer's visit coincided with a delivery from J. Westwater, Wholesale Confectioner of West Stanley. This shop, with Fell House next door, was in South Terrace at the bottom of the Fell Bank.

THE WHOLESALE CASH GROCERY COMPANY. Jack Lowther owned Lowther's Garage in the 1920s and also this small chain of five shops until the 1930s. Groups of shops like this bought food in bulk in an attempt to be competitive. The bargain buy advertised on the window was, 'Finest Marrowfat Peas, only 9½d per quarter stone.' John Cavanagh was grocer's boy here in the early 1920s. He earned 7 shillings (35p) a week plus tips for an 84 hour week, and remembered pushing 28 stones of deliveries up Harras Bank to Portobello. This shop was on Durham Road, near the police station.

WALTER WILLSONS. Mr Johnston the photographer has parked his car outside Walter Willsons on a busy day in Durham Road. The shop nearest to the camera, No. 14, the Birtley Press, belonged to Norman Ward. On the other side of Walter Willsons is Lewins' fish and chip shop. Lewins were also general dealers and hauliers. Rabbits are hanging up beneath the Lewins' sign.

T.H. ROWELL, DURHAM ROAD. Complete outfits could be bought at these shops and special clothes sent to the dry cleaners. The enamel sign indicates that Rowells were agents for Pullars of Perth the dry cleaners. Crowded window displays such as this one dating from about 1914 were more welcoming than the latest London trend introduced by Gordon Selfridge in 1909. A dramatic display of a few high quality goods was lit until midnight for the benefit of window shoppers.

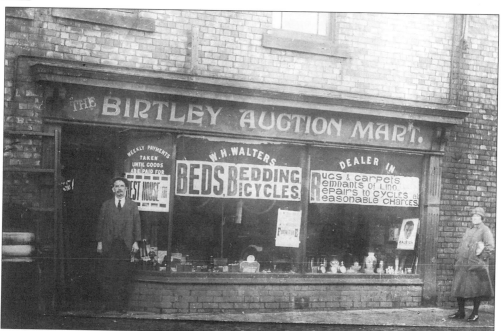

BIRTLEY AUCTION MART. Mr W.H. Walters, second hand cycle dealer, stands proudly outside his shop with its wide variety of goods.

Five

Places of Worship

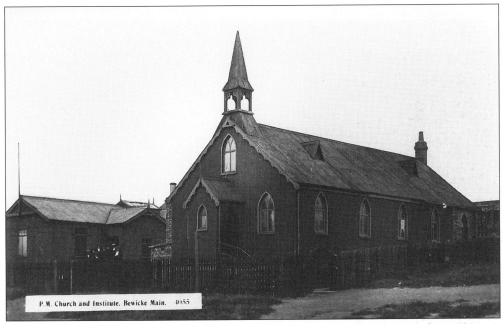

P.M. Church and Institute, Bewicke Main.   4055

BEWICKE MAIN PRIMITIVE METHODIST CHURCH. This chapel, opened in 1901, was built partly of bricks and partly of corrugated iron on land bought from the colliery owners for one shilling. At the laying of the foundation stone, members and friends bought bricks for a shilling and had their initials inscribed on them. After the last service, held on 10 April 1938, the chapel was sold to an undertaker, but it was burned down on 5 November 1938. The Institute was also built on land bought for a shilling.

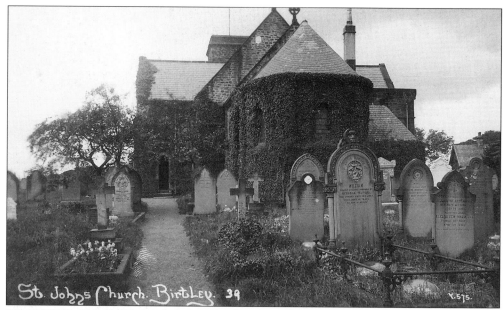

St. Johns Church. Birtley. 39

ST JOHN'S CHURCH. Birtley's Parish church, dedicated to St John the Evangelist, was consecrated in 1849, until that time worshippers had to attend Chester-le-Street Parish church. In 1847 the Revd Francis Brewsher set out from Chester-le-Street to begin independent work in Birtley. The achievements of 150 years ago are being marked by anniversary celebrations in 1997-99.

PARISH CHURCH, INTERIOR - BIRTLEY. (485)

THE INTERIOR OF ST JOHN'S CHURCH. This is how it looked in the early years of the twentieth century, but changes have taken place both inside and outside of the church since these photographs were taken.

ST JOHN'S VICARAGE. This romantic view, with a strategically placed wheelbarrow, shows the lovely building in its wooded grounds. The vicar stands at the door and the postcard dates from 1916 when Revd L.L. Barclay – previously a curate at Pelton – was the incumbent. Other aspects of the vicarage and its grounds can be seen elsewhere in this book, as it was the venue for some large gatherings in Birtley.

THE PRESBYTERY. The presbytery was built in 1870 at a cost of £1,100. Priests not only cared for spiritual welfare, but deplored the deficiencies in physical surroundings. One occupant of the presbytery, Father Phillipson, remembered Birtley as it was on his arrival in 1884: 'The population of the place could not be less than 1,500 to 2,000 souls, yet the village or township had not an inch of pavement or a solitary street lamp! There was no drainage and no water supply! It could not boast of a single pillar box.'

ST JOSEPH'S CHURCH. The growing Roman Catholic community in Birtley needed a church, and in 1841 Father James Joseph Sheridan was called to the mission. By 1843, due to his business acumen and zeal, this church was opened, followed by a school and other facilities for the Roman Catholic population. This Auty card dates from before 1910.

INTERIOR OF ST JOSEPH'S CHURCH. Roman Catholics had a mission in Birtley as early as the seventeenth century. The number of Roman Catholics was increased by the influx of Irish labourers who found work in heavy industries and as navvies in the 1860s when the Team Valley Railway was constructed. They were attracted to an established Roman Catholic community and many sent for their families to join them. This card, posted in 1906, was produced by Bealls of Newcastle who still have a stationery business in Gallowgate.

ST JOSEPH'S PRIZE BAND. They were winners of 17 firsts, 6 seconds, a 3rd prize at Crystal Palace and 24 special prizes in 1913. The smartly uniformed band poses in the grounds of The Grove and proudly display their awards. For some years, from the 1920s onwards, they practised at the Band Club on Harras Bank.

THE SALVATION ARMY BAND. The work of the Salvation Army began officially in Birtley in 1924. The first Salvation Army Hall was in the former Catholic church in Elisabethville (see p. 13) and the first officers were captain and Mrs R. Holland, two converted gypsies.

PORTOBELLO PRIMITIVE METHODIST CHAPEL. The Methodist Society started with meetings in a house, then unusually in a public house known as 'Nicholson's Long-room'. This chapel on a hill-top was opened in 1884 to seat 114 people and cost £246. It is shown here after its closure.

BIRTLEY OLD CHAPEL. On 26 March 1743 John Wesley preached at Birtley, 'surrounded by colliers on every side.' He probably preached on the old Stock Hill where Perkins' Monument now stands. The Methodist Society continued to grow in Birtley until this chapel opened in 1832. It stood in Chapel Yard near the village green and was replaced by the Durham Road chapel in 1883.

DURHAM ROAD WESLEYAN METHODIST CHURCH. This was built on land which belonged to Lord Ravensworth. The foundation stones were laid on 19 July 1882 and over £100 was raised that day, the whole cost being £1,400. The church was planned and built by Mr W. Thompson and consisted of a chapel with spacious Sunday Schools and vestries underneath. The opening ceremony took place on Saturday 10 March 1883. Although the building was demolished in the summer of 1969 the site is still open to the public on Sunday, but as a supermarket! This and the next photograph are by A.R. Hutchinson.

THE INTERIOR OF THE DURHAM ROAD CHAPEL. In March 1933 this Wesleyan church saw a series of special services and events to celebrate its Jubilee. Preachers and scholars from the 'Old Chapel' were invited to speak, there was a Public Tea, costing 9d and a lecture 'It serves you right' for 6d. Mr J.M. Lawson spoke about the history of the old chapel. The finale was a Saturday evening concert given by the Married Men's Choir when a silver collection was taken. The organ was once played by Reginald Foort – he completed the Minute Waltz in 58 seconds!

STATION ROAD PRIMITIVE METHODIST CHURCH. The 'Ranters', as the Primitive Methodists were known, first met in Simpson's yard, near St John's church, and their first chapel was built in Orchard Street in 1867 at a cost of £700. The second chapel was built in Station Road at a cost of over £3,000. A minister's house was built in 1904, costing £634, and an organ was installed in 1906. This hand-coloured postcard, sent as a birthday card in 1905, shows the new chapel set in a green field. Jubilee Celebrations are planned for 1999.

MEN OF THE PRIMITIVE METHODIST CHURCH. From left to right: Mr Taylor, Mr J. Dodds, Mr J. Smith, Mr Lee, Mr T. Hudson and Mr J. Robson. Mr Hudson was presented with a hymn book in 1918, 'As a token of appreciation of his loyal and valuable service as Society Steward for the long period of 25 years.'

BIRTLEY PRIMITIVE METHODIST CHOIR. Taken in 1917, this shows the choir of this advanced, musical and lively church. Fourteen-year-old Alfred Whitmore is at the far right in the front row. Representatives of other well known families are on this photograph including members of the English, Knox, Bolam and Allison families.

MR. KNOX, GENERAL MANAGER.

MR FRANK KNOX. This Primitive Methodist preacher was also the general manager of Birtley Co-op and a JP. As a child he was an enthusiastic member of a Temperance entertainment group, 'The Lifeboat Crew'. The activities of a Methodist chapel gave many members confidence and they used their ability in public life. Some became Councillors, Trade Union Officials, and Committee Members of the Co-op or other organisations in their community.

BROWNS BUILDINGS OLD CHAPEL. Following a revival of Methodism in Pelaw Grange in 1881, congregations became too large to meet in a house. The members asked the Colliery Company for permission to use an unoccupied cottage. This was granted and the Company also undertook the repairs and alterations. This preaching-place opened at the end of 1881.

BROWNS BUILDINGS PRESENT CHAPEL. This is how it is was described in a Jubilee Handbook in 1923, celebrating fifty years of the Chester-le-Street Wesleyan Methodist Circuit. The chapel closed in 1970.

Six

Transport

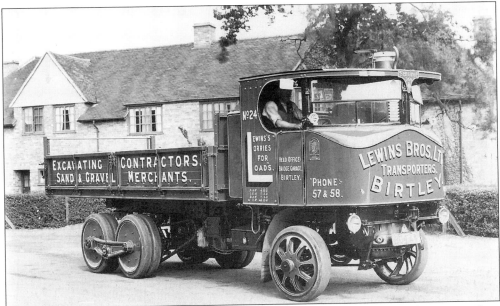

LEWINS' LORRIES FOR LOADS. This new steam Sentinel type DG6 is shown travelling from the Shrewsbury works on trade plates to Birtley, with an unladen weight of 9 tons 10 cwts. Note the chain drive.

THE ENGINE 'BIRTLEY'. This photograph appears by kind permission of D.G. Charlton. 'Birtley' was an 0-6-0 saddle tank operated by Pelaw Main Collieries. It started life around 1871 as a 2-4-0 well tank, built by Hawthorns and Co. Ltd of Leith, Midlothian for the Caledonian Railway. It was scrapped in 1928.

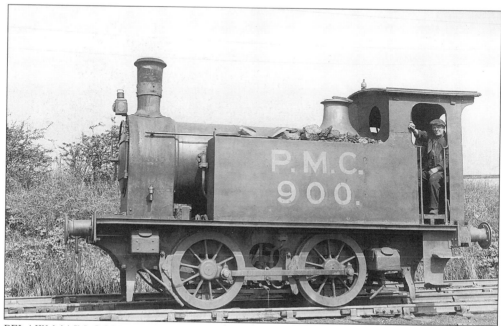

PELAW MAIN COLLIERIES. This 0-4-0 tank engine was built in Gateshead in 1888. The driver is George Atkin who lived in Birtley all his life. PMC 900 was scrapped in 1947.

BIRTLEY STATION. This postcard in Johnston's 'Monarch' series is postmarked 21 February 1925, when George W.R. Wentworth was station master. It is taken from the island centre platform, looking north. Even with two 'up' and two 'down' lines the station would be very busy especially in the summer season. Traffic coming from north and south could be diverted to the Annfield Branch.

HENLEY'S CABLES HEAD SOUTH. A.R. Hutchinson's photograph shows a Class J39 0-6-0 locomotive heading south out of Henley's private sidings to join the main line with a consignment of Henley's cables.

BURNETTS OF BIRTLEY. The Burnett family came from Yorkshire and were established as building contractors in Birtley in 1866.

PELAW GRANGE SAWMILLS HORSE AND CART. The sawmills were located to the north west of what is now the Drum Industrial Estate, and belonged to Smith & Co. The driver is Jack Armstrong and the horse looks to be decorated ready for a show.

THE MOTOR BUS. This Gibson of Gateshead postcard was posted to Calais, France on 28 August 1917, and has an Elisabethville postmark. Passengers are boarding at the junction of Durham Road and Station Lane, possible for a journey to 'The Town' from the Low Fell Tram Terminus.

BEDFORD BUS. This was operated by Crown Coaches which was formed in 1946, and like a lot of others was a combination of bus companies, one being Nicholson of Washington. Crown Coaches' address was 'Crown House, Birtley'. They were taken over by Northern General Transport in 1951. Other bus operators were Robbins of Birtley who, as 'Direct Bus Services', ran between Chester-le-Street and South Shields via Springwell, but soon cut it back to Springwell. They were taken over by Nicholson in 1933. 'General County' buses ran from 1927-36.

LEWINS BROTHERS. The transport contractors fleet is lined up outside the Coach and Horses, Birtley. They include Sentinel, DG6 and DG4 models, Leylands and Thorneycrofts. Knox and Prior later became partners in the firm.

LEWINS, KNOX AND PRIOR. A Super Sentinel is going full steam ahead in August 1937 carrying an excavator 'cross carriage'. This method was used for quick loading and unloading as it was not necessary to uncouple and recouple the trailer. Excavators such as these were used for the removal of clay in the Birtley brick yards.

TURBINIA IN BIRTLEY. This *Newcastle Chronicle* photograph shows the stern end of the *Turbinia* in the parking area of Pickford's Old Bridge Depot – now Komatsu. The stern end was sent from the South Kensington Science Museum in 1960 to the Newcastle Science Museum at Exhibition Park so that it could be rejoined to the bow section after restoration. In October 1994 Pickford's Industrial, Birtley moved the complete *Turbinia* – 103 ft 9 in long – from Exhibition Park to its new gallery at the Discovery Museum, Blandford Street, Newcastle.

PICKFORD'S BRIDGE DEPOT. This fine photograph shows a Scammell ballasted tractor. The vehicle is in full Pickford's paintwork of Pickford's blue with white lining. Its fleet number is 7063 and the 'hungry lion' is on the door. It is pulling a three-axled drawbar ex tank trailer.

A TANDEM LIFT. This railway bridge over the A6127 was built in 1903 to replace a level crossing. The railway ran to Ouston 'E' Pit. Here a W.C. Mundy crane from North Shields and a Pickford's crane, only a few yards from its Bridge Depot, do a tandem lift.

REMOVING THE BRIDGE. This *Northern Echo* photograph shows work in progress. Looking south, through the bridge, are the Crown Hotel and the Traveller's Rest, which have, like the bridge, disappeared.

ADAM ATKINSON. Adam Atkinson was one of the main road haulage contractors for Durham Chemicals which is the location of this photograph. Advertised on the vehicle's headboard is a nightly service from Newcastle to London.

HAVING A WHALE OF A TIME IN BIRTLEY. This unusual picture shows a British Road Services wagon carrying a whale! We have no idea where it was going! Behind this can be seen some of Adam Atkinson's wagons. The building on the right is the Newcastle-upon-Tyne Zinc Oxide Co. Ltd (Durham Chemicals) and the building on the left is Durham Cables, officially opened by Lord Londonderry in 1937. Norman Dawson was director of both companies. Durham Cables was taken over by Henley's in 1945, but stayed at the Edward Road site until the new works opened at Newtown in 1950.

CAWTHORN AND SINCLAIR. One of the North East's major transport companies, Robert Cawthorn and Keith Sinclair had their road haulage depot on Durham Road for over thirty years. This was on the site of the former Swinburne's Brickworks. The driver, Keith Turner, is with a Mercedes unit in its Continental livery hauling a couple of Caterpillar 435 scraper bodies.

LOWTHER'S ADVERTISEMENT, 1959. (See p. 126.)

JOE LEE. This Thames Trader van was used for furniture removals, but Joe Lee also had a coal and coke business. The registered office of this was his home address in No. 7, Newcastle Bank, although the vehicles were kept in Mary Avenue, Birtley.

THE BIRTLEY BYPASS. A Pickford's vehicle is heading south with sub-station test equipment on the Birtley Bypass. This opened in 1937 but it had to be resurfaced after the Second World War due to the damage caused by military vehicles which had used it as a parking area and as a convoy dispersal zone. Note the cycle lanes on each carriageway. The railway bridge carried the Pelaw Colliery Waggonway from Ouston Collieries to Pelaw Main Staithes on the Tyne.

ROY'S GRATE SERVICE. The company started in 1915 and traded from No. 10, Cuthbert Street, the area now occupied by the swimming baths. After the deaths of Harry Roy in 1957 and James Roy in 1962, the business was run by four grandsons, James, Laurence, Harry and Allan. Other slogans on the coal Autobaggers were 'Roys, Great for Grates' and 'Roys, Fifty Years of Grate Service'.

ANOTHER CATCHY SLOGAN. With the decline of the coal fire and industrial coal boilers, Roys started a bulk oil delivery service in 1972. They named it ROYOIL and put a crown above it, although it was not to our knowledge 'By Royal Appointment!' The business was operating out of Beaconsfield Terrace at this time and in 1974 they opened another depot at Routledge Burn next to Kellett's brick yard. When the firm finally sold out to a London company in 1986, Roys was the biggest coal business in the North East, employing fifty people and running thirty vehicles.

Seven
Industry

BEWICKE MAIN LODGE BANNER. Four famous leaders are shown with local man Ben Oliver (bottom left) who was a checkweighman of the lodge.

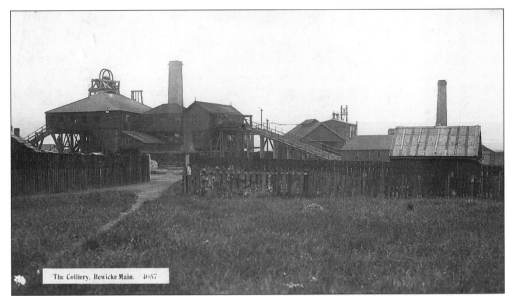

The Colliery, Bewicke Main. 4057

BEWICKE MAIN COLLIERY. The shafts were sunk in 1862 by Charles Perkins and Partners and the village was built close to the pithead. The highest tonnage figures were 141,515 in 1880 for the colliery itself, and a combined total of 173,264 in 1909 when the Mill and Riding Drifts were open. The Mill Drift was closed in 1915, the Riding Drift in 1921. The end of the colliery came when the Six Quarter Seam was closed in 1931 and finally the Low Main and Hutton Seams in 1932. By then Bewicke Main was owned by Pelaw Main Collieries.

Ouston 'E' Colliery. Birtley.

OUSTON 'E' COLLIERY. Ouston 'E' Pit, sometimes referred to as 'The New Pit' was a Pelaw Main Colliery under French control until the collapse of France in 1940. It closed in June 1940 and re-opened in 1946, passing to NCB Northern Division No. 6 Area on Vesting Day, 1 January 1947. It finally closed in January 1959 and a few of the buildings still remain on the West Line Industrial Estate.

BLACK FELL COLLIERY. On the left is the engine house with its boiler house, and on the right the Vale Pit which closed in 1932. The trucks are marked P & JR for Pontop and Jarrow Railway.

BETTY ANN PIT. This was owned by Pelaw Main Collieries. On the left of the picture are the miners baths, at that time on the west side of the A1. This area is the site of the Gateshead Angel Sculpture.

HOLDING UP THE TRAFFIC. Sixty years ago this was a familiar sight but hard to believe today. Pelaw Main Colliery wagons are crossing the then A1 with a solitary vehicle waiting to continue on its journey. The last set to travel over the Great North Road did so on Saturday 13 November 1937.

PELAW MAIN COLLIERY WAGONS AND WORKERS. The increase in road traffic resulted in a tunnel being built under the road. The first set of coals which travelled through the new tunnel is shown here on Sunday 14 November 1937 on its way to Teams Colliery. Joe Tate is the wagon rider and George Atkin (see p. 78) is third from the left.

H.N. MARSH (PLANT SERVICES) LTD. This photograph was taken about 1960 when Jack Magee and pupils from Birtley St Joseph's Senior Mixed School went into Birtley at lunchtime to record their surroundings to display on a pie chart. Marsh Plant Hire opened new premises in Birtley in 1960, having outgrown their Team Valley works established in 1953. Now the story is in reverse, Domnick Hunter Ltd, world renowned filter manufactures, occupy the site on this photograph and have expanded on the Team Valley Trading Estate.

JAM FACTORY WORKERS. During the First World War the Birtley Hall (see p. 115) became the Belgian Arcade, but it stood empty from 1918 until the early 1920s. Then part of it was used for a jam factory and the other part was used to garage buses. After the demise of the jam factory the whole building was used to garage buses and wagons. Again it became empty and was going to be pulled down when it was reprieved and re-opened as 'The Apollo Cinema'.

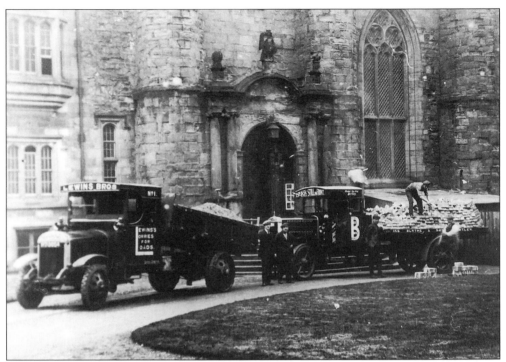

WORKING AT DURHAM CASTLE. Two famous Birtley firms, Lewins and Blythes, deliver building materials to Durham Castle in this photograph from Durham City Library. The castle was restored in 1934/35.

SWINBURNE'S CLAYHOLE WORKERS. The firm of J.F. Swinburne and Son was in existence from 1852-1938 and produced mostly common building bricks, tiles and drainpipes. These workers look particularly cheerful.

SWINBURNE'S ADVERTISEMENT. Placed in Kelly's Directory of 1934, this advertisement promotes the 'Birtley' brick. The firm closed in 1938.

TOMMY BLYTHE. This producer of Blythe's Birtley Bricks was known to be a hard working, hard drinking and colourful character. The firm of T. Blythe produced bricks at their Station Road Brickworks from 1858-1978. A layer of clay covered the coalfield in the Birtley area which was ideal for brickmaking.

THE BLYTHE FAMILY. Members of the Blythe family expanded the business. In 1931 the firm produced fifteen million bricks a year and the bricks went all over the world. Some of Blythe's wire-cut advertising bricks can be found locally, particularly from the reign of Edward VII. They bear the King's head, the firm's name and the date.

CENTENARY

1858   1958

BLYTHE'S
BEST BIRTLEY BRICKS

Ye House of Blythe
100 YEARS OLD

"The Bricks that will endure
as long as Bricks are used"

NOW AVAILABLE:

THE HOLDFAST BRICK
Specially keyed for holding plaster

Write, call or phone for full particulars

BLYTHE & SONS
(Birtley) LTD.
BIRTLEY STATION BRICK WORKS
BIRTLEY, CO. DURHAM

Telephone: Birtley 8 and 9

ONE HUNDRED YEARS OF BLYTHE'S BRICKS.

BIRTLEY IRON WORKS. This postcard view of Birtley Iron Works and Foremans Row was posted in July 1904. The works were founded in the 1820s, taking advantage of the still revolutionary methods of iron smelting. Birtley Iron Works supplied material for the High Level Bridge over the Tyne, opened by Queen Victoria in 1845.

THE BIRTLEY CO. LTD CRICKET TEAM, 1956. The team shown here is on Henley Cables' sports ground. Front row, left to right: Tom Hook (maintenance superintendent), -?-, Howard Irons (chief jig and tool draughtsman), Peter Grieves (metallurgist), Bob Burroughs (specialist welding engineer, later Caterpillar plant manager). Back row: Ray Bruce (accountant), -?-, Lish Parker (fabrication foreman), Bill Neville (draughtsman), Les Gowland (planning engineer), Norman Robson (works engineer and new product engineer with Birtley Co. and parent company BSA Ltd, plant engineer for Caterpillar Newcastle Plant).

BUILDING SCOUT CARS. The production of the Birtley Iron Company during the Second World War was geared to the war effort. Here, armoured car bodies are being produced, but field gun suspension gear and Bailey Bridges were also made.

OPERATING FLY PRESSES. Women were required to work when age and family circumstances allowed. The outcome of the Second World War depended on the maximum effort from everyone.

THE NEW FACTORY. In 1947 the Birtley Company Ltd signed an agreement with the Caterpillar Tractor Company, USA to manufacture scrapers and bulldozers to their design and specification. In 1956 Caterpillar bought the premises and started building a new factory.

SCRAPER MANUFACTURE. The 'A' building is complete and scrapers are in production. They built drawbar 435 and 463 scrapers to be hauled by bulldozers, or scraper bodies to be hauled by articulated units.

PROUDLOCK'S. On the left is the Cart, Rolly and Carriage Works, on the right the Horseshoe and General Smithy. C. Proudlock's premises were on the site of Lowther's Garage (see p. 126), now ATS.

THE WHEELWRIGHTS SHOP AT PROUDLOCK'S. Wheels were in great demand at this time as there were so many horse-drawn vehicles on the road. Skilled craftsmen were employed in large numbers in comparison to working life today.

MAKING CHEMICAL BARRELS. Coopers are seen here in the 1930s making barrels at the Newcastle-upon-Tyne Zinc Oxide Company Ltd. William Nealings was the master cooper. This firm manufactured a wide range of chemicals for the paint, tyre and pharmaceutical industries.

THE BARRELS IN USE. A large consignment of chemicals leave the NZO works, Birtley. This order must have kept the coopers very busy!

DURHAM CHEMICALS. Durham Chemicals started off as NZO, coming to Birtley in the 1930s and providing much-needed work at a time of industrial depression. In 1947 the NZO changed its name to Durham Chemicals. This firm had their own excellently equipped laboratories and a large research and development area. To the right can be seen a well-appointed sports and social club for football, cricket, netball and small bore rifle shooting. The works are now part of the Harcros Chemical group.

PENSIONERS OUTING, 1983. Retired workers from Durham Chemicals were, along with husbands or wives, treated to a free outing with meals once a year. The trips were to York, Gilsland and the Lakes, amongst other destinations, and were very much appreciated. John and Lily Hall are near the centre of this group. John Thompson, then managing director, is fourth from the right.

MADE AT BIRTLEY. This advertisement shows the new Henley's factory built on former boggy land at Newtown, Birtley. Henley's were Royal Warrant holders.

AN AERIAL VIEW OF HENLEY'S CABLES. Swinburne's clayhole can be seen on here, it is now the field between the golf course and the main road at Barley Mow.

THE OFFICIAL OPENING OF HENLEY'S. The Birtley works of W.T. Henley's Telegraph Works Co. Ltd was formally opened by the Right Honourable Lord Lawson of Beamish, Lord Lieutenant of the County of Durham on 16 October 1950. Lord Lawson was MP for Chester-le-Street from 1919-49 and held other government posts. He was Lord Lieutenant from 1949-58. He is seen here in the centre of the picture talking to Mrs Joan McKinlay on a tour of the works. Mr Cygnel, the director, is on the left.

THE BLACKSMITH. Herbert Soulsby – known as Dick – is shoeing a horse. He was a blacksmith at Proudlock's (see p. 101).

HAY RICK BUILDING. Hay ricks are being built at North Farm near Birtley around 1900. Mr Auld is on the cart and Jim Humphrey is on his right.

Eight

War, Peace and Celebrations

THE TANK BANK IN BIRTLEY. A tank arrived in Birtley in March 1918 for Tank Week which aimed at raising money for the war effort. 'Every 15/6 brings Victory nearer', was the slogan to promote the sale of War Bonds. By the end of the week £100,000 had been invested locally. In the Second World War, Birtley and District Warship Week – 18-25 October, 1941 – aimed at raising £25,000, the cost of a motor torpedo boat. A Great Opening Parade, with the Charles Perkins' Monument as the saluting base, started a week of special events, 'Full Speed Ahead for the Birtley Torpedo Boat.' By 1945 this and other campaigns had raised a quarter of a million pounds in the Birtley District.

Unveiling of
BIRTLEY WAR MEMORIAL,

On Saturday, August 4th, 1923, at 2=30 p.m.,

BY

Lieut-Colonel PHILIP KIRKUP.

■■■■■■■■■■■■■■■■

They fought so brave until the last,
I hope you will never let their memories pass.

Ever remembered by their families and comrades.

A SOUVENIR POSTCARD. Birtley War Memorial was unveiled by Philip Kirkup on the 9th Anniversary of the declaration of the war. Philip Kirkup was awarded the Military Cross in 1916 and the DSO at the age of twenty-four in 1918. In 1917 the Birtley Hero Committee presented him with an inscribed gold watch – still in the possession of his family – in recognition of the award of the Military Cross.

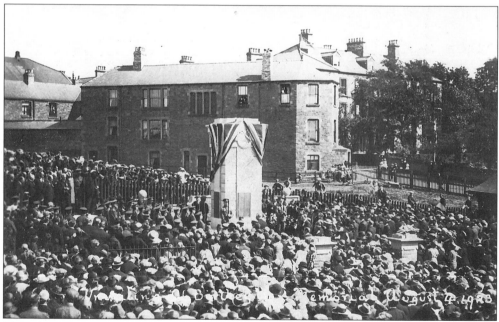

THE UNVEILING CEREMONY. The procession left the Recreation Ground at 2 p.m. and was headed by the St Joseph's and Urpeth Colliery Bands. After a religious service the Memorial was unveiled and dedicated. Residents of the nearby houses had a grandstand view. A souvenir programme was sold for one shilling.

BIRTLEY WAR MEMORIAL. A draw for War Savings Certificates raised £1,900 for the building of the Cenotaph and shelters. Mr G.L. Collins donated 500 certificates and 50,000 tickets were sold at one shilling each. The square Cenotaph was in Heworth Stone in ashlar, and the names of the 189 fallen were inscribed on bronze tablets on three sides.

COMMEMORATING THE DEAD OF THE SECOND WORLD WAR. Lord Lawson attended the re-dedication of the War Memorial in 1950 when names of those who had died in the Second World War were added. (*Durham Chronicle* photograph.)

THE HARRIS BOYS. Mr Robert Harris photographed his sons, David and Robert, after the Second World War in the back yard at Bertram Street, Birtley. The boys are now both doctors practising in the North East.

CELEBRATING THE END OF THE WAR. This street party in Morris Street was an expression of relief and joy that the Second World War was at an end, and typical of celebrations all over Britain.

SHADONS HILL BONFIRE. A typical celebration bonfire at the time, this elaborate structure was built to celebrate the Coronation of King Edward VII and Queen Alexandra in 1902.

PARISH OF BIRTLEY.

Celebration

OF THE

CORONATION

OF

King Edward VII.

AND

Queen Alexandra.

JUNE 26th, 1902.

Official Programme.

CELEBRATIONS IN THE PARISH OF BIRTLEY, 1902. There were events arranged for young and old, accompanied by the League of the Cross and Birtley Temperance Prize Bands.

LABOUR COUNCILLORS. Taken by Fillinghams of Durham and thought to be in the late 1940s, this photograph includes, back row, left to right: Dolly Morris (Pelton), Stan Hunt (Clerk to Birtley Parish Council), Mrs Hogarth, Mary Richardson (Grange Villa), -?-, and partly shown, Emma Elliott. Front row: Mary Sanders, Hannah Garside, Lady Lawson and partly seen, an unknown lady.

CORONATION PARADE, 30 MAY 1953. This took place on the Saturday before Coronation Day and was the biggest parade in the history of Birtley. It consisted of over thirty sections, from contingents of the Armed Forces to fancy dress entrants and pit ponies. Large crowds watched the colourful procession which started from the Miners' Welfare Hall. The saluting base was outside the Co-op, and the salute was taken by Lieut-Col. F.G. Slater. He was supported by Councillor L. McKie, chairman of the Coronation Committee, Councillor F. Hoggarth, vice-chairman and Mr S. Hunt, Clerk to Birtley Parish Council. The photograph was taken by the Mobile Photo Service, Newcastle. A week of special events was rounded off by a Floodlit Pageant, presented by the youth organisations of Birtley, on Saturday 6 June.

Nine
Sport and Leisure

THE ENTRANCE TO THE RECREATION GROUND. Opened on 5 April 1913, the Recreation Ground commemorated the 1911 Coronation of King George V and Queen Mary. The purchase of four acres of land, formerly known as The Grove Estate, plus a cottage and the cost of labour came to a total of £2,050. The opening ceremony was performed by Mr F. Knox, chairman of Birtley Parish Council. A poster announcing the opening is on the gatepost.

THE BANDSTAND. Published by the Birtley Press, this card was sent in 1916 by Rudolphe, a Belgian, to a lady friend in Cambridge. He says that he is doing well and works for a factory inspector. At the opening of the Recreation Ground in 1913, Mr Lancelot Moses presented this bandstand, which cost £103. In return he was presented with an inscribed gold watch by members of the Parish Council. The inscribed stone on the base of the bandstand is preserved at The Grove, his former home. It reads: 'Presented to Birtley Parish by Lancelot Moses Esq 5 April 1913.'

THE SWINGS. The Recreation Ground was for all the family. The swings were, of course, meant for children, but adults apparently enjoyed them too. A rather mature boy is sitting on one swing despite the signs which say (GIRLS) CHILDREN ONLY and (BOYS) CHILDREN ONLY. •

DURHAM ROAD. Birtley roller skating rink is in the centre of the picture. The rink opened around 1910 to cater for the roller-skating craze and it was reached by entering a tower, going along a covered corridor and down some covered steps. By 1912 trade had dwindled due to the high cost of admission, one shilling plus hire of skates. This Birtley Press card was posted to Belgium in 1916, by which time the skating rink had been transformed into the Birtley Hall.

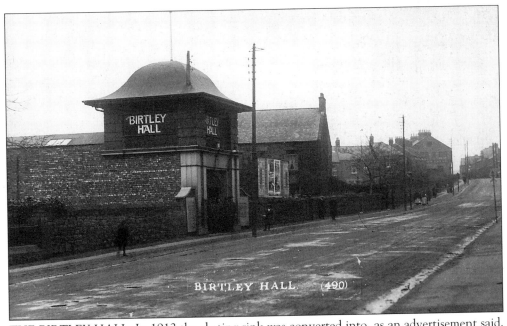

THE BIRTLEY HALL. In 1912 the skating rink was converted into, as an advertisement said, 'A magnificent picture hall, with splendid seating accommodation, only the best pictures will be shown – a place where you can confidently take your friends.'

BIRTLEY TOWN PRIZE BAND. The band and their cup are at Birtley Station in September 1908. They practised in the Station Hotel.

SHOOTING PARTY BEHIND THE HANLON. This was taken not long after the end of the First World War. The man with the moustache in the front row, holding the pigeons, is Philip Whitmore, fishmonger. The tall man behind him, wearing a buttonhole, is Mr Brown. The man on the extreme right is Mr Robson of the Three Tuns (see p. 126). The man with the moustache and wearing a hat, on the left of the back row, is Mr Hall who was a butcher and a bonesetter.

THE SONS OF TEMPERANCE. The officials of Birtley Sons of Temperance are shown here in 1910. This organisation was a Friendly Society and a Temperance Order. Every member had to sign a pledge of total abstinence. 'I hereby pledge myself that I will not make, buy, sell, nor use as a beverage, any spirituous or malt liquor, wine or cider.' Funds were raised by entrance fees, fines and contributions to pay out sickness and funeral benefits. The 'Demon Drink' blighted the happiness of many families and Methodists particularly supported temperance movements. The chapels provided alternative entertainments to pubs and clubs, they held concerts, magic lantern shows, lectures, parties and outings. Lemonade and ginger beer were served instead of alcohol and Temperance Bars provided a meeting place for those who did not wish to patronise public houses.

BIRTLEY GOLF CLUB. Col. E.H. Kirkup presents a medal to Mr J. Hedley in the 1920s. Other members include: S. Hutchinson, Golf Club Secretary (on the left with hand on knee), Mr R. Rutherford the undertaker (with cigarette and golf bag over his shoulder) and Mr Hall (on the extreme right).

THE CRICKET PAVILION. This Gibson card was sent to London from Room 5, Bloc 9, Belgian Village. Local photographers did well out of selling a large variety of postcards, especially to the Belgians from 1916-19. People did not want to send the same picture twice so anything and everything was photographed. In 1920 the annual subscription to Birtley Cricket Club was 10/6, but apprentices under 21 paid only 7/-.

BIRTLEY SECOND CRICKET TEAM, 1937. Back row, left to right: I.W. Morrison, -?-, S. Chisholm, Tom Nairn (wearing cap), T. Beadling, E. Findlay. Front row: -?-, -?-, F. Alderson, J. Chisholm, D. Whelans.

BIRTLEY TOWN FOOTBALL CLUB. Jack Robson is third from the right in the middle row, wearing a smart overcoat and scarf. The photograph was taken around 1920 next to the main gate of the former National Projectile Factory.

ROF BIRTLEY 1ST XI, 1938-39. Back row, left to right: Arthur Grimwood, Jim Kirsopp, -?-, Horace Foster, Ernie Shaw, Bob Nairn, Jack Hull, Alf Gallon and Tim Healy (gandfather of the actor). Front row: -?-, Charles Meakin (captain), Arthur Kay, George Bell (goalkeeper), -?-, Jim Malcolm.

BIRTLEY ROF FOOTBALL TEAM. Possibly dating from 1949 – George Bell is the goalkeeper, Bob Harland is second from the right in the back row and Wilf Barrass second from the left. Dennis Lightfoot is second from the left in the front row.

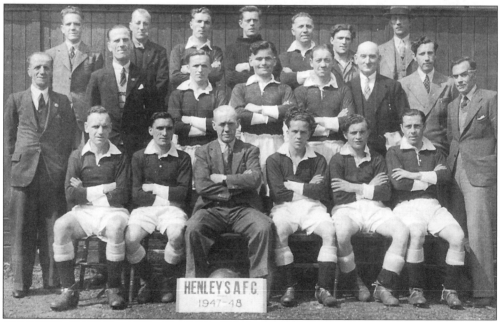

HENLEY'S SOCIAL AND SPORTS CLUB. This photograph was taken by Mr A.R. Hutchinson on the occasion of a charity match to help the Birtley Aged Miners' Scheme. The guest referee was Hughie Gallacher, the former Scottish International and Newcastle United footballer. Henley's won the match 2-1 and raised £8 8s 4d for the Birtley Aged Miners' Scheme.

OPEN AIR SWIMMING BATHS. In the 1930s the Distressed Areas Commission gave 80% towards the cost of an open air swimming baths only. The Council had hoped to build covered baths with recreation rooms and indoor bowls. In 1939 money became available for roofing the baths, but this was prevented by the outbreak of war. Many swimmers have memories of the debris in the pool, notably leaves from the 'Big Tree' and shivery recollections of the unavoidable cold shower on leaving the pool. The site of the baths is now occupied by the fire station.

THE OFFICIAL OPENING OF THE BATHS. A group of officials and swimmers, 22 July 1937. It is believed that these were the first baths erected by a Parish Council. They held heated, chlorinated water which was changed every few hours. The board says that on this day the temperature of the water was 76 degrees and that of the atmosphere was 72 degrees. By 1964 the baths had still not been roofed and the estimated cost was by then £64,000. It was decided to replace the baths by a modern indoor 25 metre swimming pool on a site opposite what is now Komatsu. This cost a quarter of a million pounds to build and opened in 1973. At that time charges were 10p for an adult, 5p for a child, and OAPs could come free as spectators.

THE OX ROAST. Mr Hindmarsh is the chef in this traditional part of the Birtley Carnival in the 1930s. Minnikins, behind the Rose and Shamrock made the coke container, the ox was sold at 3d per slice. The carnival, which also raised money for charitable causes such as hospitals, provided a week of entertainment. There was a competition for the best dressed shop, shows (including Murphy's Roundabouts), boxing matches behind the Legion and a procession of floats and jazz bands.

KAY'S TRIPS. This fleet of buses signalled that Kay's trips were off to the seaside. Birtley children were given a treat, very much enjoyed when most people were not able to afford holidays in the late 1920s and '30s. One boy remembers being given a bag of food and 6d to spend. He spent this on a clay pipe and a stick of candy rock, as presents to take home, and an ice cream for himself.

BRITISH LEGION TRIP, JULY 1950.
Ready for a day at South Shields, the
trippers pose on the station platform for the
photographer from the *Shields Gazette*. This
was the first trip after the war. Before the
war they had travelled by bus on Kay's
trips. Vera Carty (nee Weddle) is in her
mother's arms at the front. She is wearing a
party hat from a 'goodie bag' given to each
child when they gathered outside the
Legion in Ravensworth Road.

BRITISH LEGION PRESENTATION. Mr Ralph Richardson, secretary from 1917-54, is being
presented with the British Legion's highest award, a Gold Badge and Certificate of Merit, by Mr
J. O'Connell, chairman. Lord and Lady Lawson are in the centre. Sid Lovers, Ned Urwin and
Ned Emmerson are also in this group.

BIRTLEY
𝕱𝖑𝖔𝖗𝖆𝖑 & 𝕳𝖔𝖗𝖙𝖎𝖈𝖚𝖑𝖙𝖚𝖗𝖆𝖑 𝕾𝖔𝖈𝖎𝖊𝖙𝖞,
AUGUST 28, 1880.

PASS FOR MEMBERS ONLY

NOT TRANSFERABLE.)

Admit *Tho Taylor*

FREE TO FLOWER SHOW AND BALL.

TWO SHILLINGS AND SIXPENCE.

DANCE OF THE FLOWERS. Gardening has always been a popular choice of hobby in this area. This pass, costing two shillings and sixpence (12½p) seems expensive for 1880, but as well as entrance to the Flower Show, the holder could dance the night away at the Ball.

WILLIAM IV. This is the old William IV at the bottom of Harras Bank, the landlady is Rebecca Raines, the brewery is Barrass and Co. The name Rebecca looks as though it was overpainted on a different Christian name. In 1902 the licensee was James William Raine. Barrass and Company started in Gateshead then moved to Newcastle, ending up in Bath Lane Brewery which then became part of Newcastle Breweries. The present William IV is a Newcastle Breweries pub.

THE COACH AND HORSES. Taken by Julien Dedrie the Belgian photographer, 1916-19, this former coaching inn is typically set back from the road. The buildings adjoining the Coach and Horses are known as Leybourne Hold. This area was originally wooded and it is said that robbers hid there waiting to attack defenceless travellers.

INSIDE THE COACH AND HORSES. The licensee, J.R. Hughes (1920s/30s) is behind the bar. A tin of Smiths potato crisps, tins of biscuits and packets of Capstan cigarettes are on the shelves on the right.

"Three Tuns" Inn & Entrance to Elizabethville, Birtley.   4274

THE THREE TUNS. Mr Johnston, the photographer, has included his car – registration number CN 811 – in the picture, and he is actually sitting in it outside the Three Tuns while his assistant takes the photograph. Just for good measure the locals have two cars to look at, they were still a novelty at this time. Two boys on the pavement in front of the Elisabethville railings are carrying something in a tin bath.

Durham Road, Birtley, looking north. 5150

THE RED LION. This Johnston card of Durham Road shows the Red Lion on the left. Further along is Lowther's original garage – 'Petrol, Tyres and Repairs' – which dates the scene around 1920. Lowther's Garage replaced Proudlock's Cart, Rolly and Light Carriage Works and Smithy. The lorry heading north belongs to Weir and Kent Ltd, Newcastle, Wholesale Tiles – maybe they had collected tiles from a Birtley manufacturer. The horse trough which had been removed from the bottom of The Avenue to the foot of Red Lion Bank now stands on the pavement on the right of the picture.

126

THE BUFFS. Charles Perkins' RAOB Club faces Perkins' statue in this photograph taken around 1910. 'Buffs' is an abbreviations of the order's full title 'Royal Antediluvian Order of Buffaloes'.

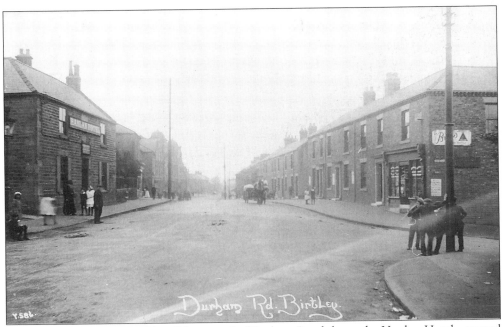

THE HANLON HOTEL. This Gibson card of Durham Road shows the Hanlon Hotel – named after a Tyne oarsman – on the extreme left. Contrast the one horse and cart with the volume of traffic on the same road today. Pedestrians need traffic lights and a crossing to safely get from one side to the other.

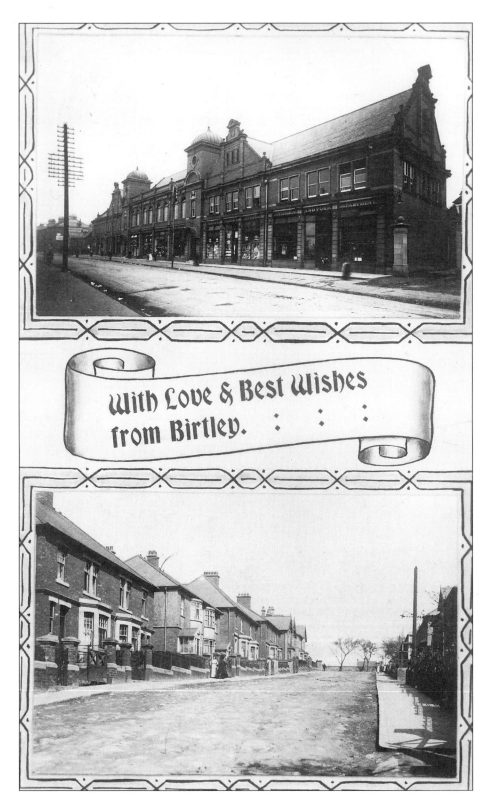

With Love & Best Wishes from Birtley.